Balancing Acts

ALSO BY ROCHELLE RATNER

Beggars at the Wall, Ikon, 2006
House and Home, Marsh Hawk Press, 2003
Zodiac Arrest, Ridgeway Press, 1995
Someday Songs, BkMk/University of Missouri Press, 1992
Practicing to Be a Woman: New & Selected Poems, Scarecrow, 1982
Hide & Seek, Ommation Press, 1980
Sea Air in a Grave Ground Hog Turns Toward, 'Gull, 1980
Combing the Waves, Hanging Loose, 1979
Quarry, New Rivers Press, 1978
The Tightrope Walker, The Pennyworth Press, 1977
Pirate's Song, Jordan Davies Press, 1976
The Mysteries, Ragnarok Press, 1976
False Trees, New Rivers Press, 1973
A Birthday of Waters, New Rivers Press, 1971

Rochelle Ratner poems

Balancing Acts

Marsh Hawk Press • 2006

06 07 08 09 7 6 5 4 3 2 1 FIRST EDITION

Marsh Hawk Press books are published by Poetry Mailing List, Inc.,
a not-for-profit corporation under section 501 (c) 3 United States
Internal Revenue Code.

Book and cover design: Claudia Carlson
Author photograph: Marjorie Cohen
Cover and title page photo, "Womb": Rochelle Ratner
The text of this book is Adobe Jenson Pro and the display is Myriad Pro.

Library of Congress Cataloging-in-Publication Data
Ratner, Rochelle.
Balancing acts / Rochelle Ratner. -- 1st ed.
      p. cm.
Prose poems about the growth of one woman or an everywoman,
from early childhood through adulthood.
ISBN-13: 978-0-9785555-0-4 (pbk.)
ISBN-10: 0-9785555-0-3 (pbk.)
I. Title.
PS3568.A76B36 2006
811'.54--dc22
                                        2006013603

MARSH HAWK PRESS
P.O. Box 206
East Rockaway, New York 11518-0206
www.marshhawkpress.org

Acknowledgments

Some of these poems, often in slightly different forms,
have appeared in the following magazines and zines:

Blazevox
Caprice
Confrontation
Hamilton Stone Review
Identity Theory
MadHatters' Review
Mobius
Muse-apprentice-guild
Poetry Bay
Poetry in Performance
Poets Against the War
Polarity
Retort
Sugar Mule
Switched-on Gutenberg
Tamafyhr Mountain Poetry
The 365 Project
The Adirondack Review
The Book of Hopes and Dreams
The Cortland Review
The Tanglewood Review

Contents

Part 1: MAKE-BELIEVE SUNSETS

Part 2: VAMPIRETTE

Part 3: SHARING THE DARK

Part 4: HOSPITAL VARIATIONS

Balancing Acts

Make-Believe Sunsets

THE VAGINA'S LIP

The vagina's lip was put there to protect her. She was a clumsy girl, terrified of spilling. She was old for her age, motherless, and she took the Ten Commandments seriously, even though this was before Charlton Heston. She wasn't the type who got crushes on movie stars or crooners. It was a fairly straightforward lip, like you might see on those orange or turquoise ceramic pitchers from the thirties, gently curving outward. Except hers curved inward. So smooth she didn't even realize it was there. She would have done anything she could to protect her firstborn, and the lip seemed to understand she would later miscarry. The daughter's born premature. And the lip is passed on.

BUILDING MOTHER

· 6 ·

Little wooden beads, like the blocks she loves to play with but never remembers to put away. Circles and squares and rectangles and diamonds and octagons and triangles and things that are just sort of weird-shaped. Thread them on a thin gold chain that feels like rain on her fingers, then put them in a glass case in the clothing store that's miles and miles away, too far to walk to and her mother always walks. Take it out so the child can count the beads, see all the different colored woods. Have a father give the woman money, have another woman wrap it up with paper and a ribbon and a gold bow. Ready now? Clasp it.

SUMMER HOUSE

"A mother is not a dust rag." SHOLEM ALEICHEM

A mother is not a dust rag, but with her hair all starched, just back from the beauty parlor, she brushes against the low pipes in the basement apartment and there are small chips of lead paint in her hair. The little girl cries to be picked up, up, up. On Mommy's shoulders she reaches out to touch the pipes herself, except she can't stay here long. She doesn't like the smell of Mommy's hair, doesn't like the feel of it. Lowered now, she puts her thumb in her mouth and sucks the dust off.

THE WORLD'S PLAYGROUND

1. Waiting to Climb the Bonsai

Like waiting for her turn at the slide. All the other boys and girls are lined up, laughing, anxious. She tries to hold her breath, smooths down her dress, prays her panties don't show. She's waiting to be the tomboy Daddy wanted. But she's small for her age. Slides and swings and monkey bars are so enormous. Climb a tree? Not even if she had to get the overstuffed cat down. That's when Grandma comes over with the small and absolutely perfect Bonsai tree, bought cheap at the end of a street fair. This is worse than the seesaw, worse than the motionless white swan on the carousel. She grabs the dusty and moldy stuffed cat and runs to hide under the bed with it.

2. Snow Day Rituals

She wears her pajamas inside out and backward, runs around the kitchen table five times, and flushes ice cubes down the toilet. Please make it snow tomorrow. Pretty please. She's been really really good. She's studied for the math and history tests later this week, she hasn't fought with her sister in ten days, and she did the dishes last night without even being asked to. It doesn't have to be a blizzard. And it's not necessary to cancel school or start late or get out early or anything. All she needs is enough snow to take her sled to the park, over behind the museum, where the older kids hang out. And please God, don't make her afraid to go down the hill this time.

KRISTALLNACHT, 1952

Picture first, if you will, a prewar building with a long, tile hallway. Small white octagon tiles, red and green near the baseboard. And two small children, the same age. Cousins. More often than not, he teases her and she ends up crying. But today they play well together. And soon Grandma's one-bedroom apartment becomes too small for their games. The door opens and they race each other down the hall and back, down the stairs and back, Grandma unable to catch them. Then, maybe to keep them near, she offers soda—Coke, Hires, maybe Nehi. No diet. No milk. Bottles made of a green tinted glass, perhaps. They finish drinking and are on the run again. More empty bottles are brought out and set at the other end of the hall in the triangular arrangement they know from toy bowling sets. He knocks down six bottles on his first try. She runs to pick them up, drops and breaks the first one.

FOOD FIGHTS I

1. Little Baker

Because her mother doesn't like to bake, a neighbor calls her in to finger the dregs from the cake batter, then the frosting bowl, hopefully chocolate. This neighbor's a heavyset woman with a daughter not much older than she is who already has a husband and a baby and is divorced from the husband and, for all she knows, might want to leave the baby, too. For this reason she's extra careful to wet her finger first, suck it clean each time, and get in every small crevice like around the rim where ants and roaches might be hiding, not that she's seen many roaches, and actually she doesn't like babies much either.

2. Chunky

The name itself should have been a warning, but what did she know? She was four years old. Her father took her with him to the barber shop, and the barber gave her one, then another, then another. Embarrassed, but considerate, her father didn't tell her till later that each of those bars costs a nickel. Same price as a large Hershey bar. But better. All those nuts and raisins. Some extra sweet gel. Chunky. She was a thin little girl at the time, one used to getting what she wanted, as much as she wanted. But chunky? Chunky. Chunky. Chunky. Everyone thought it was cute back then.

3. The 39¢ Hamburger

Daddy drove the car right up to the window on that April Sunday. She was eight years old, and Daddy was excited. There was a new McDonald's franchise where he'd eaten lunch that week, mother and daughter simply had to see this. He ordered three hamburgers, and three large Cokes. But this particular little girl wouldn't touch that glop. Her eating habits were, to be polite, unfriendly. She only ate hamburgers without the roll, picking up the meat with her bitten fingers. She didn't want any part of pizza or hot dogs. Daddy shook his head. Once again she'd disappointed him. On the way home they stopped to get her half a pint of chocolate ice cream.

4. In Sickness and in Health

Pasta will always be comfort food. Soft, bland, lining her stomach, easy to digest. *Pisketti,* as her childhood friend called it. With Butoni Marinara Sauce straight from the can, or maybe heated. Or just with butter and cheese. That melts in your mouth not in your hand and doesn't hurt your teeth or burn your gums. And more cheese. Tastier going down than she expected. Like Gerber's Junior Strained Sweet Potatoes. In the body it turns to sugar, which might be why she craves it. Stupid body. Her father's prediction of diabetes with every twelfth piece of candy. Her mother's flying spoon.

5. Boiling Water

She could have saved Grandma's life, you know. She could have boiled water. And she could have had more chicken. She could have bought the whole chicken like she promised. As she was going out the door, her final words, a whole chicken. Now the breast is gone. A little girl screams. She boils water, now that Grandma's dead and she has only one breast she boils water and pours it over tuna, like she'd read somewhere. Thinking to fool herself.

NEIGHBORS

First there was the family next door, two boys older than her who'd still come and play sometimes; she called their mother "auntie" and she remembers they moved away on her birthday. Then there was the family in the house next to that, with the first pug she ever saw and was briefly afraid of. There was the teacher who drove her to high school every day, and the girl down the street who wanted to join the Ice Capades. Then there was the gardener. No one ever asked his name, he was just "the gardener." Out working in front of his house every spring and summer day it didn't rain, never wearing anything. Over twenty times some neighbor had him arrested, but a week or two later he'd be back out there furiously weeding, without even sunblock on. In winter no one saw him, but there was talk about stealthily digging up his whole lawn, replacing it with ugly red stones that cut your feet. Someone started a rumor about poison ivy.

SILLY PUTTY

It's a blue and white egg and she holds it in her hands. You know the way she loves to play with boxes, open, close, open, close. The bottom half is blue. Open, close. Her parents bought her this. Inside is silly putty. Sort of like clay, but it bounces. Clay with a mind of its own, and a smell of its own. It will stretch unbroken, out of the cracked egg. It will stretch like taffy, like the band in her underpants. Stretch, bounce, stretch, ball. Curl it up in its fetal egg again. It's robins' egg blue, baby blue, and plastic. What's inside is magic. It bounces on the floor then flies up and hits the ceiling, or can be thrust so hard against her bedroom wall that Mother Goose tilts. Silly, her mother says. Putty, her father says. But she will not be molded.

IMAGINARY FRIENDS

She wants a white rat or an ant farm but instead she gets a parakeet, various goldfish that she never names, and a half-dead chameleon from the circus. Her cousin wets the mouth of a fuzzy dog puppet lying in a shoe box and insists he's alive (proved because he's drinking, see)? This is before the rabbit. Raisin, as they name him, is a black rabbit another cousin needed for some science project, now can't keep. Two neighborhood boys come over just to see him, then play catch with her. She learns a girl two blocks away also has a rabbit, and they share stories. The girl's older, but nice to her. Raisin dies. She takes a clear plastic shoebox, fills it with water, and puts a red plastic duck inside, telling the kids he has to be real because look, he's swimming. And they laugh at her.

FOREVER

Man. Woman. Birth. Death. Infinity. She watches Ben Casey reruns faithfully, goes to third grade, does her arithmetic homework, on winter weekends goes ice skating and learns to skate in figure eights, her favorite. She almost, but not quite, knows her eight times table, and plays with an eight-inch Ginny doll who has blonde hair and, like her, turned eight six months ago. Other than that, she's a quiet child. The sort of little girl who'll grow up to wear subdued colors and love to lie back, close her eyes, and see bright reds, greens, or purples flowing up and down her legs, skating figure eights in her pelvis, always eights lying on their backs, steadfast and moving at the same time. She wants to believe this will last forever.

DANCING WITH SCHOOL CROSSING GUARDS

Dancing with school crossing guards might have been fun had she known how to dance. Instead she trips over her feet and is too self-conscious to hear the rhythm. Walk three steps out in the street then look both ways. Too short to see over cars, third and fourth graders her size at least, she isn't a guard she's just on the safety patrol, guarded by the captain and the lieutenant, older girls. Girls she has to dance with. Then they say she's not looking, say she doesn't see, and take her badge away to the theme of exit music. She dips. Turns. Swings Pinocchio round and round and round as the elastic slips from her slippers.

THE SUICIDAL PARAKEET

The suicidal parakeet might have been drawn to the suicidal teenager, but at the time she was still a child. And even though she threw a tantrum when anyone tried to dress her up, it never dawned on her Chirpy might mind. Besides, a friend was over, and she didn't have many friends. Later, anorexic, this whole scene will make her think of turkeys, stuffing the dead bird, which often had giblets in it so she wouldn't touch it. There were a lot of things she wouldn't touch. Not, unfortunately, the parakeet, who was alive then, at least till he flew out the door or window, she forgets which. Later one dog would be killed and she'd teach another to bark *Helll-low*, which he actually learned sort of. As a puppy he was as skinny as a rat, who needed her. Unfortunately he didn't need her enough. That's why.

REALITY TV

1. Cartoons

Still in white flannel pajamas with bright yellow smiley faces all over them, she curls into a ball on the couch and watches cartoons. It's Saturday morning. Somewhere in the world she lives in it will always be Saturday morning. She's not 6, she's 16. But it's Saturday morning, Mom and Dad are at work, and she doesn't want to go shopping for lipstick or cashmere sweaters. She doesn't want to go and get her hair done. She watches cartoons. If she could just get back there, the relatively happy little girl watching cartoons, and go forward again, from there, in her mind at least … Superman leaps tall buildings in a single bound and Casper no longer frightens her.

2. The Virus

Used to be, when she had a virus, she'd lie on the pink brocade sofa with its high arms that, when she was feeling better, she liked to jump off. The dachshund would stretch out smellily on her lap while she watched This is Your Life and Queen for a Day. The Millionaire told tall tales of people given an anonymous million and how they reacted to the sudden wealth. Sort of got you hopeful. A million was a lot of money then. And there was no such thing as the Lottery. Today she watches over 200 channels on her computer screen, in a separate window, while scanning news of the latest celebrity murders or entering expenses in Quicken. There's a table that can be placed in front of a sofa the very same color as that childhood sofa, itself in front of the window, so she can enjoy the breeze, but there's no dog. Maybe there was never any dog. Just the smell of one.

MAKE-BELIEVE SUNSETS

Orange, she thought, just might be bright enough to trick her parents, make them think there was sun in her pink-walled room. She bought orange floral bedspreads, one for each twin bed. She had the flimsy orange café curtains drawn tight, then pinned together. She pulled the shades down behind the curtains, and she didn't put them up when the sun peeked in at the windowsill. The bright orange globe of one chintzy lamp shone from the stand beside her bed, a second globe perched on her desk. Then she had them remove one bed. Light crept in on her, there seemed to be light wherever she wasn't looking. Pink walls closed in on her, blotting out the orange, telling her you're a girl, you're a pretty little girl, smile for the camera, good girl, look at the birdie, try not to blink when the flash goes off.

BARK ONE, BITE TWO

Pretend it's knitting: knit one, purl two, knit one, purl two, knit one, purl two... That's what her mother, who could barely knit herself, was trying to teach her that summer. To get her interested in something, anything. Cooking. Bookkeeping. Makeup. Nothing worked till they got to the knitting. By the time she was bored she'd knit six sweaters. Nothing much else to wear, not that it mattered. Then she turned to writing rhymed poems. She found a list of markets and began to submit them, five in an envelope, always with return postage. Then she got a box at the post office, riding her bike there first thing every morning, before the breakfast she didn't feel like eating. You're making a mistake, her mother said, throwing away all that money. So she went back to letting her mail be delivered — rejection after rejection as the days grew hotter, every day more humid. And the mail seemed to come later every day, and she was crazed from the rejections, so she resorted to whatever she could do to protect herself, running out and barking, biting the mailman on the left buttock. She'd meant to just nip his ear, but she wasn't tall enough.

LATER

Day after day she would pass their house on her way to and from grammar school. The house with the beautiful lawn, her mother used to call it. When she ran away from home and walked to school and back (the only streets she was allowed to cross by herself), she'd see the father out playing catch with his two sons, younger than she was. She envied those boys. Their father taught at the local junior high, and later she would be in his class for math and English. He was the sort of teacher who romped on his large, pristine lawn with both his sons and didn't worry about ticks or grass stains. A teacher who mowed the grass himself. Later, he would start a day camp. Later still, he would murder his family.

Part 2

Vampirette

WARM WATER, GENTLE CYCLE

1. Grandma

No matter what her parents say, Grandma loves her. Grandma
tells her real life stories and lets her eat a whole pint of coffee ice
cream. When she stays over she sleeps with Grandma in the big
double bed. Grandma fluffs down her pillow. Grandma sits with
her till she falls asleep. Grandma takes her to the Ice Capades
and out on a great big sailboat every summer. Grandma brings
her home with no panties on, having simply forgotten them.
Grandma never raised a little girl before. Bye, bye Grandma.

2. Shopping with Mother

To the first store, two dresses to try on. To the second store,
where there's one dress. To the third store, where at first they
don't see anything they like, but later find two dresses. Back to
the second store, where she models the one dress again and tries
on two others. Back to the first store, then the third, then the
first, then the second. Luckily, they live in a town that doesn't
have many stores. Back to the first store, then the third, then
home, where she tries on the chosen dress once more so Daddy
can see it and Mommy sends her to bed without dinner for
announcing she doesn't care what she looks like.

3. Little Girl

And maybe, if her mother hadn't detested sewing, taking a puff
from her cigarette every third stitch, or else munching chocolate,
yet insisted on hemming every dress then letting the hem down

a quarter inch each time she grew, the little little girl would be taller now.

4. Active Wear

Even the Service Dog's dark brown coat bears a message: *don't pet me, please. I'm working.* Strange how we garb ourselves and others, the mini-skirt saying *kneel*, the halter top saying *Up, boy.* She wears stretched-out stretch pants. Grandma wore stockings with their seams always a little crooked, at least to the child's eyes. Oh, but she'll learn soon enough. The dresses she had to wear to school back in the Fifties, the knee socks with rubber-bands like corsets. She'll learn soon enough. Oh, but she didn't learn, did she? Petting fur the wrong way, year after year, one dog dead, one growling.

5. Dressing for Dinner

Because she's wearing a brown and white checked shirt, she orders meatloaf, or maybe prime rib *au jus* (if it's a fancy restaurant). And white wine. Red wine might be better for her health, but its stains intimidate. She tries to eat leaning over the table, so the food that slips off her fork will just fall back on the plate, but she's too short to lean properly. Solid colors are out of the question. She feels too conspicuous wearing red or orange, so spaghetti's nothing more than a childhood memory, like jacks and tinker toys and chocolate ice cream. They'll serve Dover Sole Almondine at her wedding banquet. If she expects to be married in a long white gown, that is.

6. *Finalmente*

The suit in which she eventually marries is dark blue, just a little darker than her gym suit. She wears it three times — to City Hall, to a cousin's wedding (Memorial Day, Virginia, 200 degrees), and to her grandmother's funeral. They were able to get out all the Bess Eaton Donut coffee stains. She even bought a second blouse, not as dressy as the white lace thing the sales associate bullied her into, but it, too, just hangs there now, taking up space in a closet as small as that junior high locker with her street clothes crammed into it during gym class (and you couldn't just wear the gym suit under your skirt, you had to change completely, and shower). All those bodies pressing in on her, the sweat, the stench, the girls with breasts already, girls with boyfriends who'd be married in long pink gowns while she was still back there trying to stay cool and calm and uncollected.

GROWING UP QUICKLY

When the bottle breaks the baby will fall... Bottle? No, that's not right. She looks again. The two-quart plastic lemonade bottle's bent at the top, as if something hard crushed it, hitting her over the head or in the shoulder as the tips of her fingers nudged it from its high shelf perhaps, like that box of Cheerios. More than just sugar-free now. It's too fat for her to get her hands around. She's too fat. At first she can't even get this bottle open, but really it's shaped to pour perfectly, tilting right into the cup. Except no drinking from the bottle this time.

REFUSE

Once upon a time she found a child's orange and white metal oven on the street and brought it home to store magazines. Once upon a time she cooked — boneless chicken breasts browned with canned potatoes and soy sauce, macaroni with butter, thyme, paprika, and parsley. Then she moved to a smaller place and the stove was left behind. She could afford restaurants now. She could heat things up in a microwave. Strange to think how that metal stove might have kept papers safe in someone's attic. Too late now, when the only toy stoves she sees are made of plastic, and she knows plastic can't protect anything. Unless, of course, some little girl, not hers but following her clear path of mouse droppings, accidentally on purpose spills water.

MAGNITUDE

Opposites attract. She fears that. She, who hated rings and beads and her mother's gaudy rhinestone clip earrings, hated doctors and their needles most of all. Thinking about mothers or doctors gives her a headache. Some days it hurts from ear to ear. But no pierced ears for her. No lace around her neck. And no engagement ring. But here, these little magnet earrings which look pierced and might help headaches and might curb appetite and won't fall off easily, see there, how good they look, her earlobe trapped between their two minuscule halves, desperate to touch each other.

VAMPIRETTE

Thumb pressure, in the right spot on the throat, she's told can kill. But little fingers give the best blood. Funny how she's come to rely on the finger that represents affectation, femininity, pretension. Everything she's always run away from. Or maybe that's why her plastic toothpick sword aims at them, because she could never run fast. Morning, noon, and night, the unlethal jabs. Baby. They used to be called the baby fingers. Unconsciously hating them, even as a child, can't wait to grow up, and the pricks always made her cry, aiming for the index finger, never suspecting it was bloodless, lost in cold thought, strident, holding onto its last drop at any cost. Even grown, she bites her nails. And the fourth finger, ring finger, the one they used to believe led direct to the heart — that one's really bloodless. Nails bitten down past flesh, she gnaws on the sides of her fingers.

IN REALITY

"In reality, he never failed to witness air spill when she unclenched fists." EILEEN TABIOS

When he clenches his fists they suck up all the air. Her throat tightens, as if she'd just eaten shellfish. Her fingers move frantically along the hem of her blue floral blouse, searching for some small thing to hold onto. With one swipe, fists unclenched, he rips that blouse off her. Now her body has room to breathe, at least, the air around her stirred for just a moment. She inches toward the door. He grabs the doorknob. Turns it. Locks it. Some day she'll go to the emergency room, but not now. It's not what you think, he won't ever hurt her. He'll spend half a week's earnings on a new blouse. She'll discover other times when it's hard to breathe. It's congestive heart failure that eventually lands her in the hospital. Her body's cranked up in the bed while he sits there, stroking the back of her hand. Three times a day they come to take her blood. *Make a fist*, the nurse says. Then, seeing how hard that is for her, offers a floppy-eared pink rabbit Beanie Baby to squeeze instead. One from her daughter's collection.

FRIENDS

I was beat up, he says. I was arrested at the peace demonstration. And she comments how surprised she is he called, knowing he hates the phone. It's been a year since they've spoken. I wanted to let people know, he says. Verbal people, unlike most of my friends these days. People who'll tell other people. You're telling me this on the phone, she says. I don't move very well, he says, jailed 20 hours and he lost 8 pounds and she asks him if and when they can get together.

FROZEN PEAS

She always keeps at least two boxes of frozen peas in the freezer because sometimes her heart runs ahead of her and the frozen peas, in their solid cold pack, are sort of like calling Halt to a horse or Stay to a dog. Little frozen green marbles on her forehead. The other pack is in case she gets hungry in the middle of the night, like she did once at a friend's house when she thought she'd been invited for dinner when the friend actually said after dinner and finally she asked if there was anything they could snack on and all she had was frozen peas which she hadn't eaten since childhood and probably those were canned peas. And they tasted good. And they laughed about it later, how given the choice she wouldn't have eaten peas but they were all the friend had and this was the beginning of a friendship that lasted ten years then just rolled away from her.

LIVING ROOM

He tells her he'll always remember the first five-letter word he learned to read: *house*. She tells him of Dick and Jane and Spot, but by the time he was in school such books were abandoned. She can't remember now when he told her this, just knows it had to be over twenty years ago. Maybe that night she drove out with him to a Seder at his in-laws'. His wife had taken a train the night before. At his in-law's *house*, she corrects herself. Or maybe it was when the two of them made three trips back and forth, Lynbrook to Brooklyn, moving God knows what to the first apartment he and his wife bought. There have been three houses since then, three places where they lived together. Houses, she tells a friend. Honest to God houses. Five-letter words he'll ever after be on the verge of forgetting.

NESTING HABITS

Deer Crossing signs she's familiar with, and even one Moose Crossing sign where she saw the moose. But here, near the swamps she can smell from miles away, a putrid smell like mother's milk, the sign says *Nesting Turtles Crossing*. She thinks of frogs ground into the tar of the road up where she lives now. Welcome to below the Mason Dixon Line. She thought all New Jersey was above that. Right. And the turtles thought they'd be safe here. She hasn't seen any as yet, still they obviously keep nesting, multiplying, crossing the road slowly, slowly, while she drives too fast. Pop goes the weasel. Splat! The turtle, with its hard shell. She thought it was a stone, or maybe an empty plastic bottle someone threw there, Pepsi or Diet Coke.

OPENING UP THE SUMMER HOME

Eighty degrees. And no power. She wakes to find three crows on the lawn. She's never seen more than an odd one here before, but there they are, beneath her favorite tree, circling, pulling something from the grass. What died here? No skunk, surely. No deer, no fox, no rabbit. And no power. Two crows squabble, then make up, their beaks somehow entwining. Three crows. A family just learning how to share. She elected to be alone here. The grass is brown in spots, despite all the snow, despite the rain. This interruption was scheduled, but for an hour later, if it didn't rain. Maybe they meant 10:30. He tells her she never takes time to read carefully. Three hundred customers, the recorded voice at NYSEG tells her. So they know the power died. What about the crows?

THE EMPTY GUEST ROOM

Betsy needs a bath. And no, she didn't wet herself. She didn't, as they say, have a little accident. The girl she was given to lost her bottle a long long time ago. Before she could blink her eyes she was carted off to the attic. Then here, to the grown girl's house, where she sits in an upstairs bedroom in the rocker that had been the little girl's once. By her side is what used to be a bride doll, maybe the very doll the girl cried for one whole weekend, purchased not at the time but a year or two later.

BALANCING ACT

Sundown, the sun in control, the earth responsive. She climbs out the window onto a little ledge, not wanting to miss a moment. She closes her eyes, tries to hold steady. But she was always a nervous child, couldn't even stand on a chair without her mother shrieking. Later she had a cat that could fall off bookshelves. Still later she bought her own house with an honest to God balcony, then later still lived in an apartment on the 20th floor, also with a balcony. Often when she's saddest about her mother's death she'll tiptoe out there. Just to think, she says. Just to reflect, like the sunset in windows. Then all of a sudden it's gone. Darkness, except for streetlights far below. The night, they say, has fallen.

Sharing the Dark

KERMIT VARIATION

It isn't easy being orange, yet oranges are her favorite. There was the tree in her in-laws' back yard, and she'll never forget how good the juice tasted that first Christmas. It's dead now, like his mother. It isn't easy being orange, small and round, and thrown like a ball by other kids on her block that summer, unwashed, unsupervised kids who probably couldn't afford balls, kids she wasn't permitted to play with. Later she dated one of them.

THE NEW LONDON BRIDGE

Because she only has eyes for him — that's what she should have said. But she barely knew him then, had no idea that twenty years later he'd still be teasing her in front of family — this crazy driving over the bridge and not even being aware of it. It wasn't a bridge she'd ever crossed before, though she'd crossed plenty. No woman's an island. Two people in his family once thought to jump from this very bridge but didn't. It's eight lanes now. It's dark out. There's a heavy guard-rail, just to deter jumpers. Her mother wouldn't drive out of town because she'd have to cross bridges — that's what she should have explained to him. But he didn't know her mother then, wouldn't have understood the idiosyncrasies passed on, or somehow avoided.

WOMEN DRIVERS

One telephone pole at the edge of an empty field, and of course she ends up against it. She's done stupid things before, but it was never this bad, never towed, never totaled. Turning into a one-way street, going the wrong way around a deserted traffic circle. She turns the car around in an alley barely large enough to walk in, never thinking of backing out. She slices off the mirror trying to get in the garage while the car in front of her parks in that first space, anxious to get in before the door comes down on her, never thinking of backing out. Just, please, don't leave me, she says to the man she'll later marry, after they've been rear-ended on the Cape. And she laughs when the brother-in-law of her future chalks it all up to women drivers. His wife comes at him with a frying pan, but her? It never crosses her mind to back out.

UPHILL, DOWNHILL

The car, to be precise, was three days old. This was their celebratory voyage, possibly the first time they'd traveled together without thought of family. Somewhere in Pennsylvania, the car having already shown its hesitation on Poconos, he and she having already argued about where to stop for lunch, the rains came. Rain so hard they had to pull off the road. Go on, she yelled, get out, pee in the trees there, get wet. She'd refused to stop for gas when she didn't need gas, he'd threatened to just pee in the car, ruin the car, which for her had died back on those hills a stronger car wouldn't even have noticed. Possibly the first time they'd really argued. Probably the last time. At least we know the car's watertight, he said. Yes, there was that to be said for it.

SLEEPING WITH A MAN WHO HAS BIG FEET

Sleeping with a man who has big feet and a hairy chest, she lets herself climb down his body, clinging, a forbidden lover roped in Rapunzel's hair. Slowly. Slowly. Hand over hand, in tiny fists, the thumbs hidden, she grips whatever she can hold. Every bone excites her. No way she can fall from here. She knows, when she reaches bottom, she'll be held there. And it gives her comfort. Finally, discovering that spot in the bed where the sheets are tucked tightly in and the quilt all but suffocates, she curls up in the foot's crotch, pillows her head on the ankle bone. This is how she was coiled sixty years ago at her mother's hard, unyielding breast. All her life she's been searching for a man like this.

VINEGAR SAUCE

It was supposed to be the salad dressing. He was supposed to
have it ready for the dinner. *Before* he went to pick up his wife at
work. But he was talking to another woman, looking at another
woman, thinking about going to bed with another woman, and
his wife's phone call, frankly, startled him. He'd forgotten salad,
let alone dressing. He ran a comb through his hair and asked the
other woman, please, to make the dressing. And what the hell
did he expect from her? She was woman, not wife. And didn't
especially care for salad. Half and half, she assumed, filling up
the cruet, half oil, half vinegar. And she shook to mix it.

BEING CATTY

She thinks, if she could just hold her claws at the proper angle, it would be all right. She'd be able to hop onto the windowsill and walk stealthily across, from sill to sill, her feet never having to touch the grimy floor. She'd just suck the breeze in, let it ruffle all her hair, not even thinking of tangles. Maybe she'd even enjoy a convertible ride, so long as its body is shiny black and there's leather upholstery. So long as they aren't stopping at Baskin Robbins. That's all they ever hold out to her — the cheap stuff. She doesn't even like the taste of ice cream. They're always trying to get close to her, chocolate covered cherries in their scratched hands, butterscotch pudding behind their massive backs. From this day on, she swears: no sugar. Giving it up for Lent, but there's always something lent. She'll curl up and let them stroke her hair. She'll maintain perfect balance and preen while the others hiss.

POUNDING

There's a hole in her head, like a bullet behind the eye, entering again and again. He wants to help her, soothe her, hold her, simply touch the tips of her fingers with the tips of his. Here's the church, here's the steeple. He wants to let her know he cares, but in this fog she can't see him. The hell with cat's feet, let him make noise when he comes. Pounding, pounding, pounding like a lobster. Like a valentine.

LAST WEEK

For her last week of wife training he sends her... flowers or a plant... she can't remember. You think it was so long ago, but nine years isn't. And the woman in the flower store where she ordered the corsage was the same woman he spoke to but she kept her mouth shut. He was wondering if she would. For her last week... They held onto the card at least, kept it on its white plastic spoke and placed it in the base of the iron tavern puzzle she'd bought him years before, two hearts intertwined. The trick is to part them.

HOME STRETCH

There was record-breaking heat the day they decided to marry, but that didn't stop the rain from pouring two weeks later and it didn't reverse her mother's stroke or stop her from having a brain tumor which ended up not being a brain tumor after all. She wanted to die a wife but that didn't stop either of their mothers from dying, or her dentist. And twelve years later it's hot again and her friends with birthdays have moved away and maybe it's a tumor and maybe not and she's twelve years older and still doesn't know what she wants but if she loses another ten pounds she wants to wear her mother's wedding ring, the one they broke stretching.

SHARING THE DARK

She wants to show him how dark it is. There are no streetlights and no other houses here. The sky is solid black on a clear night with just a crescent moon. But his father leaves the car's headlights on. So they'll find their way. She wants to point out the Big Dipper, so clear in this sky, and Sirius, the dog star. His father's seen all this before. She wants to share the dark with both men in her life. But his father, having just lost his wife, doesn't want any part of it.

MARS

It was the 1950s when she attended Hebrew school, the middle of the Cold War and the race for outer space. They used a series of workbooks called *Rocket to Mars*, probably still somewhere in her parents' attic. But she grew to hate Hebrew school, and was never bat mitzvahed. She might never have married, either.

*

Her seventh grade teacher lived next door to a man who set up telescopes in the middle of the street. She remembers stopping there with her father as a child, before she'd met this teacher, before she grew up, before her father retired, before he took sick, before her mother died. He was interested in the heavens then. Tonight he says he read about Mars in the news, thought maybe he spied it through the car window.

*

In the dark, alone, she searches the skies for that glowing reddish light three days early. Just in case she misses it.

*

Think of the *mar* that is marriage. They thought she'd never marry. Then she met him. The old problem solver, accustomed to doing things on his own, who doesn't need her help and yet doesn't reject it. Call it *love*, not help. At 6:00 a.m. this year, on the very morning of his birthday, Mars will be closer to earth than it's ever been before. But he's not some little green man. Like it or not, she's from New Jersey. And she won't be with him.

THE NIGHT SKY

Confetti, she thinks. Glowing confetti, or fireworks. Up there in the lights over Trump's casino. Small, brilliant objects floating across the sky. And no, it's not a star. It's something like she's never seen before. These casinos, she thinks, will try anything for a little summer business. She knows this town. She was raised here. Now she tries to show it to the gambler. But it's not the same. The two amusement piers, her favorite part of childhood — gone. But there are still rides, further up on the Boardwalk. They cuddle in an old wicker rolling chair. They take a roller coaster, single cars, shaped like a mouse. He goes on a $20 rocket experience, twice. From the Ferris Wheel they see those objects again — gulls, hundreds of them, crazed, almost hitting against the highest rides. The tilt-a-whirl makes her nauseous.

THE WRONG SIDE OF THE BED

She's been away for two months. Now it's another middle of the night. It's raining out. She wakes from a dream she's too tired to remember and has to go to the bathroom. She starts to swing one leg over the side of the bed, a ritual she's been following for seventeen years, and hits… and hits… not the wall, not wood… the bed's Formica sideboard! She can see the lights of the city vaguely reflected. She traces the disk of her watch, a tiny circle, as it moves one palm's length ahead of her. She lifts her legs free of the thin summer blanket, crawls to the foot of the bed, then angles out past the treadmill, using its handlebars for the final hoist, vaguely smiling, determined not to be upset by this, careful not to wake him.

DOG

He says it was the huge, long-haired, grey or just grungy dog prostrate on the porch. Right where people are walking. She tripped over the dog, he tells her. Could happen to anyone. And he's right there to hold her up like he held her up on the ice the night after they married and like he held her crossing the midtown street. People will think she's drunk, she says. And he says enjoy it. The dog lifts its head and looks around in confusion. It's the second time she falls. Or rather the third time, but don't let the dog find out.

LOUISVILLE

The house Pomeranian doesn't bark at night, not that people would mind much, it being New Year's Eve. Everyone at the Victorian bed and breakfast gathers for champagne at midnight. No Pomeranian. Tomorrow they'll tour the race track and find the Louisville Slugger factory closed. No house Pomeranian. Her beagle puppy came from Louisville. The dead Pomeranian.

ANYWHERE

Her first night in Houston was also her last day somewhere else. It could have been anywhere. A city, perhaps. A place with traffic and pollution and taxi cabs. On her way to the airport the cab was leaking oil and the traffic was heavy and the fumes engulfed her. A headache started that lasted through Christmas despite all the love and all the presents. At the very mention of Houston that smell returns. Even in her own car, windows tightly closed, the smell reverberates. Her fuel. Her car. Her nostrils. But it could have been anywhere.

DRILL

The jackhammer's right by her head. She wants a taxi. Stands, to hail it, a foot off the curb. In the sun she can't see if the light's on. The jackhammer's two feet away. She hears nothing, doesn't understand why the cab doesn't pull up in front of her. It becomes a test of wills. Her husband says she never sees. Dust three inches thick on the table. Camouflage, she calls it. All she knows is the sound of the dentist's drill. How scared she was. How, tender lover, he promised to stop the minute she raised her hand.

MURMURS

1.

At least it's not a voice, she said. At least it isn't whispering at
her to do things. Been there, done that. And he was beside her
then, purposely taking the side with the ear infection. Then
letting his voice drop. Been there, done that. Another little voice
said she could love this joker. Maybe.

2.

At least it's not a voice, she tells herself. She sits on the porch at
night and can't tell for sure if she's hearing the bullfrogs call to
each other or if it's just her. Wishes now for that old refrigerator
so loud it blocked out the other country noises. The day after
it was junked she realized that if she had her left ear to the
pillow she couldn't even hear the birds. Right's her weak side,
she supposes—broken arm, breast cancer, a wrist that still
hurts, the eye only 20–10 with glasses. Not the side with the
wedding ring.

3.

At least it's not a voice, though as a matter of fact talking might
help. Concentrating lets her ignore it, or driving, washing dishes,
hanging curtains. If she can just keep herself busy she knows
it won't speak to her, but at two a.m. it's so quiet. Even words
like *brain tumor* might be welcome now. Funny to think of it,
though, his never saying I'm wrong, or I'm sorry.

GOING TO BED ALONE

Whenever she sleeps with her lover she doesn't wear anything, so it's just as well he's out of town. Or in town, actually, she's the one who's away for the summer. As far away as she can get from noise and drunks and streetlights. So when the speeding car leaves the road, clips a telephone pole, ruptures a gas main then, airborne, crashes through her bedroom wall, flies over her bed, then partly out through the bathroom wall, pinning her under it only momentarily, its tires leaving deep impressions on the mattress but her body sinking even further (it's one of those pillow-top mattresses), she's virtually unharmed except for cuts here and there, but she's extremely glad she has an old T-shirt and panties on.

HOT DOG

There's a hot dog with a battery in it. From the stand he loves, on 86th St., or the cart on Flatbush. Nathan's even. It doesn't matter where. Two hot dogs with sauerkraut and mustard—the mustard hides the real taste, the sauerkraut coats the stomach lining, much like bread or milk does. Well, let's say they've run out of sauerkraut. You know, how they caution, batteries must be properly disposed of? And don't subject to heat or they might explode? It's 95 degrees out there. She can look at his mustard-smeared hands and glimpse the future. She sees him, tomorrow, calling from the hospital, about to undergo gallbladder surgery. He'll tell her he's been in and out of pain for months. She's not the sort who notices such things. Were it not for those two hot dogs with their little bombs inside he might be in pain forever and ever. Amen.

FOOD FIGHTS II

1. Hole Chicken

Hole Chicken, the white foil-lined wrapping says. She's used to buying roast chickens in their plastic tubs, the top clear so she can see the skin's crispness. What does it have to hide? A bullet hole? All chickens have holes, or cavities, for the stuffing, and she never trusts that stuffing doesn't have giblets, regardless what they say. She doesn't need this chicken, or any other chicken. It was just an excuse to get in the car and drive alone down country roads right before it got dark with the radio blasting. Usually by eight o'clock they're sold out of chickens. Maybe that's why they wrapped it. *Hole chicken.* Like a golfer's hole in one, like the hole in someone's argument. Don't ask who. And she can't stand golf, out in that hot sun all day. With the wrapped-up chicken in the front seat of the car, she takes the short way home, the radio suddenly not as all-encompassing. She sets it on the table, juices leaking, and unwraps it to find the skin perfect, the flesh so tender it falls apart between the prongs of the fork. A little dry, perhaps, but still excellent. Also, while she was out, her husband called.

2. Candyland

On the two-hour plane trip they played a game, alternately naming some particular candy — Clark Bar, Almond Joy, Snickers — until one of them couldn't think of any more. She won, but inadvertently cheated. He gave her a box of Russell Stover chocolates that year — jellies, nuts, and creams his brother picked up for him at the nearest drugstore open on

Christmas morning. He'd had a "more thoughtful" present, but with stress on the job, then last minute packing, left it sitting on his desk. They passed the candy twice around the room, then she ate the rest. *Blimp*, he called her tenderly, after the Goodyear Blimp which made Florida its home. They'd been together five Christmases, married for better or for worse, in health and in sickness. But what, she wonders, if it happened now? Doctors strictly forbid her eating sugar. The Goodyear Blimp crashes two days after her birthday.

3. *Lunch*

She wonders if it's okay to use cinnamon sugar substitute in pureed butternut squash, like she does with mashed sweet potatoes. She picks up the bottle. Were her husband here he'd be laughing at her constant need for sweets. She starts to unscrew the lid, then decides to just open the little pouring latch. She looks at it. Thinks again. Then, just at the moment she starts pouring a wind comes up and blows it all over the table. She pours more in the squash. She uses one wet finger to gather up what's on the table. She mixes the squash, then mixes more, eats. The cinnamon seems to congeal on the bowl's rim. This being lunchtime, her being alone, she wonders if it's okay to lick the bowl.

4. *5:00 A.M.*

Because she just found out that salted pumpkin seeds are actually still in the shell and you're not supposed to eat the shell. Because she didn't start in on them until after three, sitting on the bed, thinking one last snack, and she'd had half the bag eaten before she read about cracking them. Because they were hard to crack. Because it took her almost the full bag to get the hang of it, biting just the tip, on the narrow end, then gently prying. Because the sheets are covered with the remains of salty white shells. Because for four nights she's gone to bed with him at close to midnight and now he's left her. Outside a bird sings.

5. Boiled Ham

After thirty years of being a typical New York Upper East Side then Upper West Side food snob, she's decided on plain boiled ham, whichever brand's on sale, shaved. She lays it out on a paper plate, sits at the table and picks at it with her fingers, rolling each thin slice carefully by itself as she once rolled Play Dough. This she does in loving memory of her mother's sister.

6. Leaves Falling

It's cold for mid-October. They're seated on the sofa, but no cheese and crackers this time, no olives, no tapenade. There are flowers and plants all around them, brought from the church service a week ago. They had a little problem last night with the falling leaves, their hostess says, as if they need reminders that no man's here to extend the dining room table. Nightmares of her father breaking the chandelier. They'll just eat on their laps, she supposes.

LITTLE CHRISTMAS

It's been one of the warmest years so far. She walks the neighborhood in forty degree weather, taking photos of Christmas trees set out near garbage cans. But the tree still stands in her living room, taking up half her living room. And the lights are still there, catching sun in daylight, glowing every night from six to midnight, red on the bottom, followed by a string of orange lights, then yellow, green, blue, the white star on top. She has no use for angels. Behind all this fanfare pine needles, turning brown, emit the familiar scent. The tree stands on its one leg in a bucket that was once full of water, but it stands tall, almost to the ceiling. Most people don't even notice it's dead.

WITH SHOVELS

Then, even though it was still drizzling, they all knelt down and built sand castles on top of the grave, vying with each other for space and that good, red dirt. She remembers when he first told her about that dirt and how proud he was. She wanted her castle to reflect that, tall and unique as a New York City pre-war building, strong enough to sustain high winds, and wives, and the groping arms of dead parents.

Part 4

Hospital Variations

ONE DEER

One deer, without antlers, darts across the back lawn and into the trees again. Had she not been eating breakfast at that very moment, looking up as she reached for her coffee cup, she would have missed it. Twenty-four years in this house, and it's the first time she's seen a deer. Twenty years ago she'd sit out by the pond in the early evening, swatting mosquitoes, begging just one deer to come. West Nile was, in those days, someplace in Africa, as far off as the deer seemed. Then she found out about salt licks. Then she found out about Lyme disease.

THE EXTERMINATOR'S DAUGHTER

1. Cartoon

I got rid of the roaches, now I can't get rid of the exterminator, the cartoon under the glass top of her parents' dresser read. That's what happened to them in real life. Only it was waterbugs, not roaches. It was long before roaches were resistant to chemicals. And the last thing either of them wanted was to be rid of each other. They almost didn't get married, though, because it was just after the war and they couldn't buy affordable furniture. Then they found this bed, chair, two night tables, dresser, and highboy set. The first month they had it she burned the top of the dresser with her cigarette. Maybe that's what the glass top was doing there.

2. The Mosquito Cop

The mosquito cop slaps her arm, and back, and cheek. Stop it, Daddy. But she's been a bad girl, eating sweets again. Mosquitoes love the chocolate around her lips, the sticky peppermint on her fingers. Hasn't he told her that a gazillion times? Daddy ought to know, he traps ants and mice and roaches. He drives around in a great big truck, spraying stuff that makes her eyes cry. She no longer rides around with him in the evenings. Daddy slaps the back of her calf. He slaps the chest that will need a bra soon. Daddy loves her. But it hurts when Daddy loves her. She'd rather have the sting of the mosquitoes. She'd rather have the itch, and the bright red scabs she can pick at with her bitten fingernails.

3. *Refineries*

Fumigate. It's the only way, her father says, to get rid of bedbugs. He remembers as a child, he and his father would go into a house, shut all the windows, tape them so no air leaked in, then set off the bomb. The trick was, later, to dart back in and get the windows open before the fumes overtook you. And his father so often didn't wait for him. He'd go to the customer's house after school and find him passed out on the floor. But this was what a son did, in those days. Fathers began a business, and their sons absorbed it. Not like today, when parents are blamed for everything. He swears his daughter's daily headaches and his nephew's allergies had nothing whatsoever to do with those fumes they grew up with. Absolutely impossible. Besides, by their childhoods even chlordane and DDT were scented, harmless. Here, smell the oil they cut it with. He and his brother even gave it to their wives, to dab on their wrists, and behind their ears sometimes. And of course her mother gave small bottles to all her friends, though her mother didn't have very many friends.

4. *All Her Life*

All her life she's been afraid of bees. Her father knows that. Then suddenly there are two bees coming toward her. She recognizes them by their orange and black stripes. No, yellow and black stripes. Very small bees. She manages to swat and kill one, but the other stings her. This is what she's been so afraid of, this tiny prick she barely felt? But then her whole body starts to ache. She worries she's allergic to bee stings, but her father says this is normal. Suddenly there's another bee, and another, then a hundred bees, and she remembers bees fly in swarms like fish in schools. She's going to get stung again and again and again. Frightened, she runs to her father, but he insists there's nothing he can do.

5. *Dead Bee*

What's there to eat on a dead bee? Plenty, she supposes, if you're an ant. Even a fairly big ant — carpenter, she thinks it is. First the ant walks round and round the bee, prodding seven times to be sure it won't sting. Then he or she mounts it. Even manages to turn it over. Can't quite tell if it's food or not. The ant walks away then returns. Burrows under one wing, for the shade perhaps. The other wing, or part of a wing, comes loose. Blows across the porch. Did she mention before there's a porch here?

6. *The Wasp Nest*

She thinks, if she positions her chair directly beneath the wasp nest, maybe she won't be stung. The wasps have been around all summer, but today's the first day she's found the nest, on the side porch, right beside the light fixture. Wasps go in and out from the little hole, but the nest itself is as large as her head, perhaps. She remembers how to get rid of wasps — you have to wait until evening, when they're all inside the nest, and then bomb it. Or is it in the morning? The word *bomb* troubles her. She wonders if it's radioactive, if it's nuclear. And does this mean she'll never have a family?

7. Country Living

While she brushes her teeth, the spider spins his web in a
corner of the large sink. At first he seems paralyzed by the noise
of the electric toothbrush, but then gently reaches out a leg or
arm or claw or whatever it is. Meeting no resistance, he reaches
out again. Halfway through her brushing his two front legs are
moving rapidly, synchronized with the motion of the brush, she
realizes. The sound, to him, must be music. Back and forth, up
and down, in little circles. She's glad now she isn't a child, to
have been afraid of this.

8. Tic Tac Toe

The worms begin a game of Tic Tac Toe in the soft wood of
the pine tree. Then the pine tree is sawed into those gorgeous
wide floorboards. A century later she buys the house and has
the painted floor refinished, and of course the game board's
filled in. Each spring she returns to find more of these lines
visible, as if carved into the wood with a penknife. Her father's
the one who tells her about the ancient worms. They seem to
have congregated in the boards selected for the bedroom and
near the kitchen table. Every once in awhile she drops a few
crumbs for them.

9. In the Door

In the door of the refrigerator, ten years old and quite possibly
no longer working well, sits a jar of cocktail sauce next to a
jar of horseradish next to a jar of peanut butter. The cocktail
sauce, mixed with horseradish and poured heavily over
large cold shrimp, is especially tempting on nights like this,

right before a rainstorm, the third day in a row she's had a sinus headache. The peanut butter is to place on mouse traps scattered all about the house, along walls, in corners. The horseradish is home-style.

10. Mouseblood

She awakens in the middle of the night to the sound of the mousetrap thumping against the tiles in the bathroom. The mouse must be caught by the leg or tail. Maybe he'll get away. She rolls over, good ear to the pillow. Then gets up and moves two cabinets because he'll stink if she doesn't. There he is, behind the statue by the kitchen door, wiggling. She hits him three times with the statue. Leaves a trail of mouseblood. What she thought was a piece of mouse fur turns out to be chipped from the statue. She forgot bricks break. Poor statue. Next time she'll know enough to use her shoe.

11. Trapper I

The mouse, who doesn't quite have his neck in the trap, just his front legs and maybe a portion of his chest, manages, when he sees her enter the room and approach him, to bounce about as many mice do, but this one manages to get the trap finally close enough to the baseboard that he can spring the lever and retreat inside the wall. She was afraid of something like this. She should have picked up that trap and dumped him outside, but it was raining. For the first time in thirteen years she wants her cat back, and she couldn't stand that cat.

12. *Trapper II*

Even as she's writing this she has a second chance, another
mouse caught in the trap in the other room. This one looks
like it might escape too, the way it's batting about like that, but
she's not going to let that happen twice in one night, and maybe
to even the same mouse though she doubts one mouse can be
that dumb and she's seen several running around here. This one
she picks up, dumps in the toilet, and flushes, but it manages
to keep its head above water and damn near climbs out when
the water's low and she flushes three times and it's still moving
its paws in that climbing motion that just might save him so
she takes the handle of a mop she never uses, which is right in
the bucket there, and tries to poke his head underwater. Damn
mouse, he almost manages to climb up the pole but in the end
she gets him. She just hopes the toilet doesn't clog now. That
was stupid except she's found other mice floating there, and yes
she could have just let him go outside but he wasn't dead and
might just come back in, tonight even, and she wasn't about to
get involved in that cat and mouse game.

13. *In a Nutshell*

The jar of peanut butter's half gone. Three years, two traps, and
maybe thirty mice, the first one this summer beaten to death
with a sneaker, six babies discovered in the bathroom drawer
and drowned. In the bedroom, by the ultrasound repellent,
a hundred ants crawl up her arm. She just hopes they don't
bite. Maybe that's why the mice have kept their distance. She
remembers tiptoeing through the kitchen, trap in hand, arms
behind her back, trying to dump one outside without her
father-in-law seeing. She remembers her mother-in-law unable

to climb the hill she didn't even realize was a hill. She had a car like that once. Sold to the friend on the left who never drives fast anyway. Yet another computer's headed for the scrap heap. Her mother-in-law's dead, her father-in-law remarried. Her father and his ladyfriend, so close that summer weekend, on rocky ground. If she didn't know better she'd think she was killing them.

14. Civil Defense

While the bugman's in the hospital, the room in which she works smells of mouse-piss. She lifts the top on the old double school desk. *Take Action as Directed*, the yellowed card reads. At one point she thought of using this for a table. *Prepare.* She vacuums up shredded paper from what was once a nest, throws out envelopes and file folders she hasn't needed in decades, comes face to face with two minuscule unblinking black eyes. *Attack Imminent.* At first she thinks he's dead. When he moves she runs for the hammer. Not the good one, but the one she never uses. Missed. *When the Warning Sounds.* She takes out the trash and sprains her ankle coming back in. This is how her father met her mother. And he's still out there somewhere.

15. Glowing Insects in Hopes of Cutting Malaria

A friend, running at night through the city, tapes strips of foil on his jacket to make sure drivers see him. And she remembers those fireflies of her childhood, some trapped in jars, others trapped in her bedroom. Every summer mosquitoes bite the hell out of her, regardless what repellent she uses or how many citronella candles she leaves burning. But does she really want to see every mosquito preening a fluorescent green as it heads for her? Swatting one mosquito's fine, but she has her doubts about making males infertile and killing off a whole population. Her father, she knows, would take issue. Just get out there and spray them, he'd say, use the strongest chemicals you can get and kill them all. But her father, these nights, says little, stays inside the house, weak and dizzy. No, it's not malaria. But it might as well be.

16. Ants At The Funeral

Ants at the funeral, marching single file along the kitchen baseboard. Minuscule ants. He's lived in this house over fifty years and it's the first time he's seen them. He didn't have ant spray yesterday so he threw bleach at them and they vanished. But they're back today, just a few of them, sharing the kitchen with a handful of mourners. Her nephew, he whispers, breaking down again, he's the one who convinced her to have the operation. Now he's here with his wife, and his granddaughter.

PRESSURE

It's atmospheric, you know. Any change in pressure. And she isn't the only one. Headache clinics hire temps just to answer the phone on days like this, neighborhood drugstores have to substitute Tylenol 3 for Percocet. It's physics, not nerves. Blood vessels don't expand or contract to adjust the way they're supposed to. Same reason ears pop and babies cry when planes rise, some worse than others. After awhile you pretend to get used to it. Sure, sure. Twenty years of dance class, and she's still offbeat. She thrusts her head in her hands and storms out into the storm, just as her father walks back in with a cold rag for her forehead. God, you'd think this was his fault.

MEN WORKING

She asks for doors this time, not open shelves. Keep the clutter hidden. Seventeen years since those old shelves were built, another seventeen and she'll be in her seventies, maybe even unable to climb the stairs. She lives in a city where signs read *Danger: Men Working.* And she knows that danger. Falling bricks, flying splinters, sparks, wind, the flu season. Over her head saws and hammers drown out the book she's reading. Directly over her. She'd wanted her desk thirty inches but the best they can do is twenty-six, in that room upstairs, in this building without coffin corners.

A DOCTOR A DAY KEEPS THE APPLES AWAY

Oh sure, she supposes she could run into the supermarket, or the Korean grocery, and buy an apple or two — waxed, with a little sticker on it describing its variety. But she's thinking here of apples from one of her two trees, out by the pond. Or of apples fresh from the orchard three miles away which often wins prizes at the county fair. Mouth-watering apples less than an hour away from the tree, as distanced as a day without medication.

THE YELLOW PLASTIC BAG

It sits, neatly folded, on the closet's top shelf, distanced from the clutter just beneath it. But it holds something small and rectangular, visible even from across the room. Something, perhaps, a little old lady was looking for. Standing on tiptoe (afraid to climb on a chair), she rummaged through the lower shelf three times. That's how it got so messy there. The bag waits patiently. It contains a book, perhaps, or a box of candy. She shouldn't eat candy, being diabetic and undiagnosed. Quietly, unseen by others, this yellow plastic bag has saved her life.

HEARTS

1.

Her heart is green, bright green, dirty green, dishrag dirty, and dripping green paint. She twists it one way then the next, wringing out some torn sweater inside it, twisting, twisting, trying to force blood up from the base of her spine, bright red and clean. Her hands are soaking. She pulls harder, makes a fist, stretches, slackens. Hearts should be bright red, Valentine red, or maybe red and green, but not struggling, the two colors in gentle harmony, especially this close to Christmas.

2.

She wears the long sleeve black T-shirt with the large white hearts tie-dyed front and back when she goes to the radiologist. She hadn't exactly planned to wear this, really it should be thrown in the hamper, but she was rushed this morning and just threw on yesterday's clothes. Not until she's in the office bathroom and sees in the mirror how the heart drapes across her breasts does she realize what she's done. Still, this has got to be a good omen. She bought this T-shirt at a sprawling flea market in Florida a few months ago and actually she didn't want the heart, didn't even see it until she was two aisles away, but she was with family and she'd lost them once already.

DON'T LOOK

Diagonally across the street from the breast surgeon's office, two men in red *EVENTS STAFF* T-shirts are standing in the middle of the street, blowing up a street fair for the rich kids. They stop to let a UPS truck through the closed-off street, then continue pumping. Early for the doctor, she leans against a pole and watches. At first she thinks it's one of those trampolines with colored balls, but of course she's wrong. It's a gigantic bowling game, with bright white bowling pins blown into an arch over the gate and huge dirty sand-bagged pins as tall as a rowdy ten-year-old that will have fallen down two dozen times by lunchtime. Not till she's leaving the office does she realize it's a human bowling ball. Or big red apple. One girl at a time is strapped inside it.

MOTHER'S MILK

Thank you for not using your cell phone, the sign at the receptionist's desk says. The nurse moves it a bit to draw attention. This is the second call a woman's gotten — the first from another doctor's office, the second from her daughter. The other daughter was just sent home from school with head lice. First in her class. And, oh my God, she was crawling all over me Sunday. Get that shampoo, quick. Change the bed sheets. Soon the lice will be gone. Soon the breast will be gone. Bye-bye.

OVERCOME

Overcome your fear of needles, the sign on Mt. Sinai's bulletin
board reads. Never has she stumbled on anything so
appropriate. There are phobia shrinks, she knows, most of them
more than she can afford. But this, at this very moment in her
life, when she needs blood tests weekly, not to mention flu shots
and boosters for Lyme disease…She writes down the place and
time, arrives an hour early. One by one, others arrive, all of them
women — chittering, chattering women. One talks of her first
grandchild, and how desperately she wants to knit him little
blue booties, maybe with tassel ties. Another talks of her sister
in North Dakota, how cold it gets there, she always thought a
nice home-knit scarf… a third woman (though she's not really
listening now) talks of a throw to curl up on the sofa with, deep
rose to match the upholstery. When the instructor arrives with
skeins of wool, she sneaks out the back door. Really, she doesn't
even want to give up her fear of needles. Times like this, it's as if
that's all she has.

FIRST DREAM, SECOND CANCER

It's ID day at the senior center — not only free photos, but hairstyling as well. Even though she's too young, they invite her. The nurse at the door whispers to come back, the only volunteers free right now have no sense of style, but she doesn't want to hurt their feelings. They sit her down, place the tabby cat on her head and he starts kneading with his claws, carefully, tightly curling. As a child, she despised her curly hair, like the rest of her body. It feels good, the cat massaging the back of her head, but then he moves around to do the front, full belly draped across her face, warm penis just about nose level. Still, she doesn't move. And her hair ends up in wonderful ringlets, except on the top, where what little is left lies limpid. This cat needs to keep others warm, you know.

SHEEP COUNTING HUMANS

Sheep counting humans. That's the last thing she remembers before going under. Not the drip in her arm that she'd been so frightened of. Not the guy wheeling her down the hall while all she could see was a yellowed ceiling, telling her how he used to drive a cab and this was so much easier. Not her husband hanging on beside her. Not the doctor with his white mask hiding his usual smile. Just sheep counting humans, and how it used to be she didn't count.

WHAT WE DO FOR BEAUTY

Seated on a plush couch in the surgery waiting room, a woman puts those old-fashioned pink clip rollers in her hair, then takes them out. One falls on the floor and rolls under the bench without her noticing. She checks her hair in a pocket mirror, unable to see the top sticking straight up. Across the street, immaculately-dressed children are being dropped off and picked up at the most expensive nursery school in the city. The eye-patch on a priest's father, glimpsed through the waiting room door, is blindingly white. In recovery, a young doctor tells a twenty-something woman that her lumpectomy went well, also giving her the name of a tattoo artist who specializes in covering scars. Mike something, he says. Out on Long Island, he says, but probably he means the Hamptons.

LIKE A FLYING SAUCER

She remembers a bright round light, like a flying saucer, hovering over her stomach as she lay there. Where? On a floor, a carpet, a table, a gurney, a sofa, a bed. She can't remember. Just that light, that all-pervasive light. Like the teenage light in her bedroom, over the recliner, on night and day. She kept the blinds drawn, the door closed, locked out both noise and love. Hotter than school in there.

HOSPITAL VARIATIONS

1. Display

They didn't have Eckerds when she was growing up here. They didn't have much of anything. Still, early June always meant beach chairs and shovels and goggles, but she doesn't recall a bright green snorkel mask and tubes. Not that she'd have noticed, hating to get even her chin wet. It costs five dollars. Probably nothing but a toy. *Play* was something else she detested. Especially beach play, her body on display. Her father's body, snorkeling, at this very moment, two blocks from the ocean, five from the bay. It's too cold for swimming. His hands are cold. His tubes are much larger than this one. And they're pale blue.

2. Eating the Sea

She gags. Spits. Gags. God, she hates this water. Still the child who couldn't swim. Daddy took her out past where the waves break, though. She liked that. Daddy holding her. Bouncing on his shoulders. Laughing. Up up up up up. Down down down down down. Spit, Daddy, spit. Daddy spits out the food that should cushion him. Without salt, he says, it's tasteless. Up up up up up. His lungs fill with water.

3. In the Cards

Two of hearts, the Keno woman calls from the lounge across the hall. His heart, her heart. All he knows or cares is that his heart is failing. Five of clubs. Five days hooked up to tube after tube after tube that he won't remember. Five of diamonds. The nurse brings a phone to his room. He wants to call her number but by mistake gives the nurse his number to dial. Nothing but a machine. The nurse calls her name, he calls her name, to rouse her. A bit more awake now, he dials her number himself. She doesn't recognize his voice, thinks this some cruel joke, hangs up. Ace of spades. His heart, alone, shoveled.

4. Tour

He tells them the reason it's so noisy here is because this window looks out on Michigan Avenue, where the Expressway is. All the cars, night and day, filled with people headed for the casinos. Can't wait to lose their money. And she tells him no, it's Pacific Avenue out there. From the window they're looking at Bally's. That's Michigan Avenue, he says. He's lived here all his life. A friend draws a map for him. He turns the map upside down. Wishes to hell they'd never built that Expressway. It feeds onto Arkansas Avenue, but pointing that out would only confuse him more. Instead, they look out the window again and name the buildings, count the Jitneys passing by, point to pigeons on the ledge below. He says again it's Michigan Avenue, with all the traffic. He's lived here all his life. From his bed, held in by tubes, he can't see out the window.

5. The Helicopter

The helicopter lands outside your window, just like the man in the other bed said it does. The same man who told you, three days in a row, he's going home tomorrow. All the lights sinking past the window. He saw it twice last night, while you were sleeping. With the curtain drawn between your beds, you circle your finger at your temple and smile for our benefit. And it's true most hospitals have helicopter pads, but on a third floor roof between ten story buildings? The helicopter whirls and spins and circles right in. Eighty-five years old and you can still see something new. You're the one supposed to go home today, then they say one more test, then another x-ray. You watch the propellers stir up dust on the rooftop, see a flash of red, get sucked into the sudden stillness before doors fly open. Never thought you'd live to see this.

6. Good Humor

She can't even eat a popsicle these days without thinking of those childhood afternoons on the beach, walking in the sand, avoiding broken shells, looking for abandoned popsicle sticks, cruddy to say the least, washing them off in the water, then trying to fit them together to form a raft, when she didn't even want to touch them. Her fingers seldom had the dexterity, but her father helped her. It's what fathers did in those days. She goes out on the screened-in porch with a creamsicle, one Good Humor novelty she detested as a child, twirls the cruddy stick in her fingers. Hard to believe she was ever that child, or he that father, 400 miles away now, clinging to the liferaft, finally floating free, but cruddy.

7. Eighty-Six

Eighty-six — coffee shop lingo, means they've run out. Of pork chops, of chicken, of flu vaccine. No, that's in the doctor's office, at the school, at the senior center where they'll go to vote. Doctors fined if they pass on the drug to those not needy. Mothers and fathers fined if they eat when not hungry. Everyone fine and dandy, until they run out. And her father definitely not fine today, eighty-six in the hospital. A nurse's voice comes over the intercom, wishes happy birthday, then they show up with a piece of birthday cake, then an insulin shot to counteract the sugar. They have no vaccine yet.

DIE

Every time he shakes the dice he hears two people brushing against each other. A man and a woman, late at night. Little black eyes inset in a milk-white face. You'd think they're dalmatian puppies. *No, never,* and *don't try to hold me back.* Those are just some of the words he hears, or pretends to hear. All bark and no bite, as the woman reassures him. Those two so close together, always together, hot from the warmed hand. He blows as if to cool them. The woman tenses. The boy he was once sits up in bed. His emptied hands feel cold, then colder.

HIS DEATH

She doesn't want to hear it, not now, not in the summer when she's staying focused, so she goes off in the car somewhere, anywhere, for dinner, shopping for food, shopping for poison, and she gets back and of course the message waits. She goes back to work, writes about him this time, sleeps on it, and in the morning it's pouring rain and she sees from her study window that she left the car window open, the window nearest the house, of course on the passenger side.

THE HEARSE

The hearse follows her into the gas station, unnoticed until after she's pumped, made sure she has the cap on, tightened it further, reached into the side window, unzipped her pocketbook, caught hold of her wallet, paid with a credit card, and chatted with the elderly woman in her booth. At first it surprises her that a hearse needs gas. Then she looks past him: only one car. So this isn't, yet, a funeral procession. She wonders if there's a casket in the back. She wonders how long he's been waiting there.

FALSE WAR, FALSE SUMMER

Look, the oak tree's dying. Bit by bit, bark peels off. The yellow ribbon slips down, looser and looser. Soggy with rain, the bow wilts. Who the hell cares, when the yellow's inside her? Not a star but a lariat, whirling, criss-crossing her gut, slowing to get a hold on. It moves up to her breasts, circles one then the other, figure eights. A decorative little heart on top of each breast. Perfectly centered. Wilting in this early summer heat. Too soon, too soon. And my God, all that greenery.

About the Author

ROCHELLE RATNER is a poet, fiction writer, critic, and editor. Her books include two novels: *Bobby's Girl* (Coffee House Press, 1986) and *The Lion's Share* (Coffee House Press, 1991) and sixteen poetry books, including *Beggars at the Wall* (Ikon Books, 2006) and *House and Home* (Marsh Hawk Press, 2003). A strong Internet presence, her e-books include chapbooks from Tamafyhr Mountain Poetry and xPressed. An issue of the Internet zine *Sugar Mule* was devoted to her writing and an exploration of her writing by others. *Hide & Seek*, an original poem-photo series based on the limited-edition poetry volume, is posted on the Light and Dust website. An anthology she edited, *Bearing Life: Women's Writings on Childlessness*, was published in January 2000 by The Feminist Press. From 1979–2006 she was Executive Editor of *American Book Review*, and she continues to serve as a Contributing Editor for that publication. She's been teaching writing workshops in senior centers and hospitals since the early 1970s. More information and links to her writing on the Internet can be found on her homepage: www.rochelleratner.com.